COBRAS!

A MY INCREDIBLE WORLD PICTURE BOOK

MY INCREDIBLE WORLD

Cobras are snakes known for their hooded necks and unique displays when threatened.

Cobras can be found in Africa and Asia, living in forests, grasslands, and near water.

One species, the **King Cobra**, is the longest venomous snake in the world, growing up to 18 feet (5.5m) long!

Cobras can raise the front part of their body and spread their neck ribs to form their famous **hood**.

They belong to a group called **elapids** that have permanently erect fangs at the front of their mouth.

Cobras' sharp fangs are used to inject venom into their prey and to defend themselves.

6

Their venom is a neurotoxin that can be very dangerous, even to us, but they usually avoid people.

Spitting cobras can spray their venom at predators up to 8 feet (2.4 m) away!

Scientists use cobras' venom in medicine to create **antivenoms** that save lives.

Cobras are **carnivorous**, eating mostly small animals such as rodents, birds, and other snakes.

They use their forked tongues to smell and find food by picking up scent particles in the air!

Some cobras can swim and even hunt for fish and frogs to eat!

They have better eyesight than most other snakes, which helps them locate prey.

Cobras are **oviparous** (egg-laying), and some species guard their nests until the eggs hatch.

Baby cobras are called **hatchlings** and have fully functional venom at birth!

Cobras communicate with other snakes and animals through their body language and hissing.

Their hiss is lower in pitch than many other snakes and can sound like a loud, deep growl.

17

Cobras' main predators include mongooses and large birds of prey.

Some cobras play dead when they feel threatened, lying still with their mouths open!

Cobras' smooth, shiny scales help them move easily through their environment.

They are important because they
help control the populations of
prey animals in their ecosystem.

Cobras are incredible!

Made in the USA
Monee, IL
29 November 2024

71533600R00017